BARNARDO'S

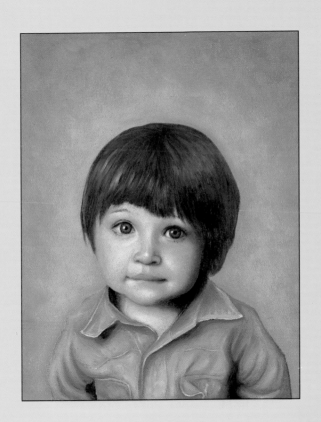

DIANE CHURCH
(SERIES EDITOR: ROB ALCRAFT)

Heinemann
LIBRARY

First published in Great Britain by Heinemann Library
Halley Court, Jordan Hill, Oxford OX2 8EJ
a division of Reed Educational and Professional Publishing Ltd

OXFORD FLORENCE PRAGUE MADRID ATHENS
MELBOURNE AUCKLAND KUALA LUMPUR SINGAPORE TOKYO
IBADAN NAIROBI KAMPALA JOHANNESBURG GABORONE
PORTSMOUTH NH CHICAGO MEXICO CITY SAO PAULO

A 3% royalty on all copies of this book sold by Heinemann Library will be donated to Barnardo's, a registered charity, number 216250.

Produced by Plum Creative (01590 612970)

Printed in China

01 00 99 98 97

10 9 8 7 6 5 4 3 2 1

ISBN 0 431 02752 8

British Library Cataloguing in Publication Data
  Church, Diane
  Barnardo's. - (Taking Action)
  1. Barnardo's - Juvenile literature
  I. Title
  361.7'632

Acknowledgements

The publishers would like to thank the following for permission to reproduce photographs:

All photographs by Paul Carr except pages 6, 7, 9 from Barnardo's Archive. Some photographs use actors.

Cover photograph reproduced with permission of Barnardo's.

Cover illustration by Scott Rhodes.

Our thanks to Barnardo's young people, families, volunteers, supporters and staff who kindly assisted in the preparation of this book. Thanks also to Sugar magazine and St Michael's Primary School in north London for their co-operation.

Thanks to Ravi Wickremasinghe, John Grounds and Ali Worthy for their support and comments in the preparation of this book.

Every effort has been made to contact copyright holders of any material reproduced in this book. Any omissions will be rectified in subsequent printings if notice is given to the publisher.

All words in the text appearing in bold like **this** are explained in the Glossary.

CONTENTS

WHAT'S THE PROBLEM?

We know that many children in Victorian times were poor, hungry and overworked, because photographs from those times tell us so. Fortunately these worst hardships are now rare in the UK. But there are still many children in the UK who have problems and need help – even though they don't wear ragged clothes.

HELP NEEDED

For example, how can you tell just by looking if there is anyone at your school who hasn't got a mum or dad? Or if one of your friends has been beaten or treated badly by a parent?

The fact is, you can't tell. These children may not work in factories or live on the streets, but they still need help.

OVERCOMING PROBLEMS

If you have problems like these, you know how these children feel. If you don't, perhaps you can imagine what it must be like. At times you would feel lonely or sad. Sometimes you may get angry or upset. You may just feel frightened. Barnardo's helps children cope with these feelings and overcome their problems, so that when they grow up, they can lead confident, happy lives.

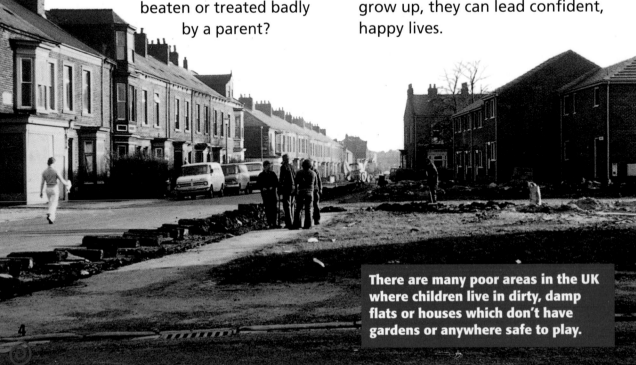

There are many poor areas in the UK where children live in dirty, damp flats or houses which don't have gardens or anywhere safe to play.

4

One child in ten is beaten or ill-treated by their family.

For their own safety, many children in poor areas are kept indoors where they get bored and fed up. Their parents can't afford to buy them nice games or toys, which would make time at home more fun.

Some teenagers leave home when they finish school, because they can't find a job and their parents don't have enough money to look after them. Many of these young people end up living on the streets. Barnardo's does its best to help them.

One child in four in the UK lives in poverty.

WHAT DOES BARNARDO'S DO?

In 1865 a young man called Thomas Barnardo visited London and was shocked to see thousands of children living on the streets. He was so angered by what he saw that he devoted his life to helping them. He opened homes so street children had somewhere warm and safe to stay. He started schools so poor children could learn to read and write. He provided training so they could get jobs and earn money. Barnardo's has worked with children for over 130 years.

BARNARDO'S TODAY

Today Barnardo's runs 250 local projects for children and families. Each project provides a different service. Some protect children who are in danger; and some find new mums and dads for children who can't live with their real parents.

Some projects provide playgrounds, libraries and quiet areas for children who live in poor areas and wouldn't otherwise have these things. Barnardo's projects are all different because children and the help they need is so different. What they share though, is Thomas Barnardo's belief that every child has a right to a loving, secure childhood.

▼ **When Thomas Barnardo started the charity he cared for children in large homes. Today Barnardo's does its best to keep children with their families so they can solve their problems together.**

Barnardo's helps nearly 30,000 children, young people and their families each year.

Thomas Barnardo helped 88,000 children during his lifetime. Because his homes and schools cost so much money to run, he spent a lot of his time giving speeches and writing letters to get people to give money.

Barnardo's runs 250 projects across the UK.

HOW DOES BARNARDO'S WORK?

As well as providing services for families and young people, Barnardo's shows the public how hard life is for some children. It produces reports and **surveys** that tell people what life is really like for some children, and suggests ways to make their lives better. Barnardo's also works with politicians – work that is called **lobbying** – to get them to pass laws to help children with problems.

FUND-RAISING

Barnardo's needs lots of money to pay for its work. Some of this money comes from businesses and local councils, but much of it is raised by people like you and your family through sponsored events such as jumble sales, sports days and collecting boxes.

The problems facing children have changed since Victorian times, but there are still many thousands in need of help. Barnardo's does its best to support them.

▲ **Many actors and sports and TV personalities help Barnardo's raise money. Some of them make donations and some of them attend fund-raising events. Frank Bruno, the ex-world champion boxer pictured above, has helped raise thousands of pounds for children.**

▶ **The glasses campaign shown here, with Anthea Turner and children, raised £222,000 for Barnardo's.**

Barnardo's has cared for 350,000 children since 1866.

> Politicians need to know more about the problems facing children if they are to pass laws to help them. Barnardo's arranges for children and teenagers to visit the Houses of Parliament where they can tell politicians about their difficulties.

In Victorian times 50 per cent of children died before the age of 10 from illnesses such as *dysentery* and *tuberculosis*. These illnesses occur when children live in bad conditions. They have recently been reported again, because the number of children growing up in poverty is on the increase.

Barnardo's raises over £80 million a year from the UK public and government.

MEET SHIVALI PATEL

I am six years old and I have a twin sister called Shivangi. Being twins, we are very alike in many ways – we go to the same school and enjoy playing together. But Shivangi has severe **disabilities**. She cannot walk, talk, or feed herself.

I really like being with Shivangi – she is very sweet. Because she can't see very well, she likes to touch and feel things when we play, so I tickle her under the chin which makes her laugh!

Sometimes Shivangi goes to stay with another family who are her **carers**. Shivangi needs looking after all the time at home – like a baby – so when she goes to carers, it gives mummy a rest and daddy more time to spend with me. We were put in touch with Shivangi's carers through Barnardo's.

This is a day with my family.

▲ Shivali and Shivangi love to play together.

▲ Shivangi was born with severe disabilities. No one knows why. She needs to be looked after 24 hours a day. Her family were put in touch with Shivangi's carers through Barnardo's Family Link project in east London. Carers look after severely disabled children for any length of time, from a couple of hours a week to several months.

10

There are 360,000 disabled children in the UK.

DID YOU KNOW?

Mothers should be pregnant for 40 weeks. In the past, a lot of babies born before 40 weeks died. Today many more can be saved. Some have disabilities, though, because they are born before they are fully developed. This has led to an increase in the number of disabled children in the UK.

8.30am Mummy drives us to school. Shivangi screeches with excitement as we arrive. She loves coming here. Shivangi and I are in different classes — I'm in Miss Jones's class and Shivangi's in Miss Clare's.

11.00am Shivangi goes to see a special nurse, a **physiotherapist**, who helps her move her arms and legs. Then we have lunch together in the hall. Shivangi has to be fed because she can't chew food or feed herself.

2.00am Shivangi starts crying and mum goes to her. Shivangi wakes up a lot in the night as she gets pains and cannot move about on her own in bed. Mummy changes her nappy and we all go back to bed. Shivangi cries again at 5.00am, but this time I manage to go back to sleep straight away.

7.30am I get up and get ready for school. Mummy is very tired because she has already been up with Shivangi for a couple of hours.

3.00pm I go home with mummy, while Shivangi goes to see Mr and Mrs Patel, who are her carers. They look after Shivangi one night a week. I like being alone with mummy sometimes. When Shivangi's there, she gets all the attention.

8.00pm I have my bath, daddy reads me a story and I go to bed. I try to get to sleep before Shivangi comes home because she always wakes me up in the night.

➤ **Shivali and Shivangi are lucky that they can go to the same school. Many children with disabilities have to go to special schools.**

Only one family in 20 with a disabled child has a carer to help them.

MEET AMANDA STERN

FUND-RAISER

If you have ever wanted to throw a wet sponge at your teacher or felt like sitting in a bath of cold custard, I'm the person to call!

It's my job to come up with exciting ideas to get people to raise money for Barnardo's.

Fund-raising is a great way to have fun and help others at the same time. If people didn't give money to Barnardo's, our work would come to an end and thousands of children would suffer.

Sponsored swims, carol concerts at train stations ... you name it, I'll arrange it. But what I enjoy most is going into schools.

Here is a typical day for me.

9.00am Back to school for me today. I'm doing the Harvest Festival assembly at St Michael's School in north London. I've brought cuddly toys, harvest festival collection envelopes and old clothes with me for the service. You never know what might come in handy.

9.15am The infants' assembly begins. I tell the children how Barnardo's started, how Thomas Barnardo rescued starving children in Victorian times and what the charity does today.

9.45am Now the juniors. In this assembly I go into a bit more detail. I get one of the pupils to dress up as Thomas Barnardo and the children agree to take part in a Harvest Festival fundraising appeal.

▲ **The school assembly is a good opportunity for Amanda to tell the children more about Barnardo's history and for them to think about other children who are less well off than themselves.**

12

School-children raise £900,000 for Barnardo's each year.

◄ Not quite Thomas Barnardo, but a good try. In the assembly Amanda explains how Thomas Barnardo once turned away a boy with red hair nicknamed 'Carrots' from one of his homes because there was not enough space. That night Carrots died in the cold. From then on, Thomas Barnardo vowed never to turn a child away from one of his homes again.

▼ 'Don't ask teachers or strangers for money,' explains Amanda. She runs many different events in schools and is used to telling children about the dos and don'ts of fund-raising, not just the Harvest Festival appeal.

11am I go around the classes explaining the appeal. 'What do I do with my envelope?', 'Where can I put my stickers?' are some of the questions I get asked. One clever clogs asks me if he can keep the money for his pet rabbit. You can guess my reply!

2pm An afternoon at my desk. A school calls about making a video on Barnardo's and a group of students, who organized a sponsored trampoline bounce, have had their photo taken by the local paper. In between phone calls, I manage to make up some fun packs to take into schools.

5.30pm I'm worn out, but I do love my job and wouldn't change a thing. I can't wait for the sponsored fancy dress disco on Sunday!

Barnardo's fund-raisers visit 4,500 schools each year.

MEET MARIE ENNIS

PRESS OFFICER

Have you ever wondered where the news stories you see on the TV come from?

The news is produced by journalists – people who work for newspapers, TV, magazines and radio programmes. As a press officer, it is my job to get journalists to produce news stories on Barnardo's and the work we do. That way people will know more about the terrible problems facing children and teenagers.

Journalists often call Barnardo's press office if they have questions or ideas for stories about disadvantaged children. It is then up to me to decide who they need to speak to and to set up an interview.

I work at Barnardo's head office in Essex with three other press officers. This is a typical day in the office.

9.00am I look through all the morning newspapers to see if there is anything about children that may be of interest to Barnardo's.

▲ **Journalists often want to talk to young people, to find out more of what has happened to them.**

10.00am The phones start ringing. The government has just made a statement about young children and its plans to teach and prepare them for school. We get calls from the BBC, Channel Four News and Greater Manchester Radio. They want our view on the subject. I tell the journalists I will call them back as soon as possible with a statement.

14

Barnardo's press office receives 2000 enquiries from the press each year.

11.00am A rush meeting is called with our Senior Director Roger Singleton. We agree to tell the press that we are very pleased that the government is looking at new ways to help children before they go to school. However, Barnardo's is worried that the plans will not provide enough help for **disabled** children and those who need special help with learning.

11.30am I type up our statement and fax it off to all the different newspapers, radio stations and television channels. Some of the journalists want to talk to Roger Singleton and I arrange for him to be interviewed.

2.00pm I get a call from a writer on *Sugar* magazine, who is doing an article about teenage runaways. She wants some facts and figures for the article. How many teenagers run away from home each year? Where do they go? I put her in touch with someone in our research department who has the answers.

3.30pm I'm rushed off my feet setting up interviews for our Senior Director on the evening news with ITN, Capital Radio, the BBC and Channel Four. I draw up a list of questions that our Senior Director is likely to be asked and suggest some answers.

5.45pm Roger Singleton is on the ITV news. He's a great success. Phew, the day's over. I wonder what will come up tomorrow? No day is ever the same in this job.

Barnardo's promotes stories in the *media* about children, young people, families and the problems they face.

21,000 children ran away from home last year.

MEET JOANNA WESTWATER

PROJECT LEADER

What's more important to you – keeping warm in winter or not going hungry?

I am project leader at the Barnardo's Family Centre in Bo'ness, in Scotland, and around here there are thousands of poor families who face decisions like this every day. They can't afford all the basics most of us take for granted: a home, food, warmth and lighting. So they have to make choices. And there is definitely no spare cash for clothes, trips to McDonalds or Christmas and birthday presents.

Living like this, at home all day with no money to do anything or go anywhere, young children get bored and parents get **depressed**. The Bo'ness Family Centre was set up to give mums and dads the chance to get out of the house and make new friends – and to give children the chance to learn new and interesting things. Here's how we do it.

9.00am The children arrive at the centre in the Barnardo's minibus. Inside the centre, it's bright and cosy. For some, it's warmer here than at home, because their parents can't afford to heat their homes.

▲ **Children of all ages learn through play, mixing with other children and trying new things. Children who are stuck at home all day sometimes learn more slowly than others or misbehave because they don't get the chance to try new activities.**

10.30am The children are busy painting pictures in the play room. It's great for them here. Paints and paper are expensive to buy, way beyond the budgets of the families here, so the family centre allows them to try new things.

Three million children in the UK are growing up in poor families.

The family centre is colourful, bright and fun. There are lots of things to do and lots of space to run around. The children look forward to their visits.

12.30pm Some peace and quiet as the children eat their lunch. Lentil soup and jelly are on the menu. A healthy, affordable meal which the kids love. Clean bowls all round!

2.00pm The toy and book library begins. The children can borrow anything they like for 20p a week. This fee goes towards buying new books and toys. It's a great system because their mums and dads haven't got enough money to buy new toys and books from shops.

5.15pm The After School Club, for children whose parents are still at work, is in full swing. Games, sports, park visits – we do anything that interests the children. There is also a quiet area to do homework.

Two-year-old James selects a book called *Each Peach Pear Plum*. The toy and book library helps children learn to read and learn new things that will help them when they go to school.

6.00pm Everyone's gone home. I have one last look around the centre and check that everything is locked up. I set off home to put my feet up.

17

Around 1.5 million children have to live in damp, overcrowded houses or high-rise flats.

WORK WITH MEMORY STORES

What reminds you of your mum? The smell of her favourite perfume, the theme from *Coronation Street*, her photo in the living room? Most of us take such things for granted, but not 10-year-old Tom. His mum is ill and won't live much longer. When she dies, these memories are all he will have to remember her by.

Tom and his mum have collected many special things for the Memory Store. Tom can keep the Memory Store forever and will always be able to look at it whenever he misses his mum after she dies.

SOMEONE TO TALK TO

Barnardo's has more than 20 projects for children like Tom, who often feels lonely and angry that his mum is dying. Barnardo's helps him talk through his feelings with someone outside the family, and come to terms with what's happening.

SPECIAL THINGS

Tom and his mum are also putting together a Barnardo's Memory Store, which is a colourful box and book where special things can be kept forever.

3000 children in the UK are affected by AIDS.

A ticket from the 1996 European Cup is Tom's favourite thing in the Memory Store. 'I went with my mum and dad and we had a brilliant day. I'll never forget when England scored that fourth goal against Holland!' says Tom.

'I'm going to miss mum a lot when she dies and it will be hard. But the Memory Store will help me remember her and help me be strong. At least dad and I will still have each other.'

▲ Tom's mum has written his life story for him. Tom won't be able to ask her questions about himself once she's died, so it's important Tom's mum writes it down for him now. Here she tells Tom about when he was born.

Tom has chosen a video for the Memory Store of the family when they were on holiday in Devon. Tom's mum has put in photos of Tom when he was first born and written about what he was like as a baby, because he'll never be able to ask her when he grows up.

KNOW THE FACTS

Tom's mum is dying of an *AIDS*-related illness. Lots of things have been written about AIDS, many of them untrue. Because of this, Tom has been teased at school by other children. This makes Tom very sad. All he knows is that he doesn't want his mum to die.

Two thirds of children affected by AIDS in the UK, are under 10.

WORK WITH YOUNG CARERS

Last year Sally got into trouble at school for not doing her homework. She was bullied by other children and fell out with her friends because she never had time to spend with them. But Sally does not misbehave, nor is she unfriendly. She is a young **carer**.

Young carers are children who look after sick or **disabled** grown-ups, as there is no one else to care for them. Usually the person they care for is their mum or dad.

CARING FOR MUM

Sally's mum has **multiple sclerosis** and she never sees her dad. Before she was put in touch with Barnardo's, nine-year-old Sally says: 'I had to do everything for mum. When I woke up in the morning I'd take mum a cup of tea and help her onto her bedpan so she could go to the loo. After emptying that, I'd get breakfast for mum, my little brother Darren and me, before getting us both ready for school. Then I'd set the machine off if there was any washing. Before leaving the house, I'd give mum a wash, get her dressed and help her into her wheelchair.'

▼ **While Sally's friends enjoyed themselves, Sally did the housework. She felt cut off from everyone. She didn't want to tell her mum what was happening because she knew her mum was very ill and relied on her for help.**

There are up to 40,000 young carers in the UK.

Sally is now much happier. She has caught up at school and is now top of the class for spelling. But most of all, Sally likes having time to play with her friends.

CARING FOR THE HOUSE

When Sally came home from school in the evening she had more work to do: cooking tea, going shopping, ironing and putting her mum to bed.

Sally fell behind at school and had no time to play with her friends. She felt lonely and very sad. Sometimes Sally got annoyed with her mum for making demands on her, but then she felt guilty as her mum was ill and relied on her for help. Sally was scared that if she told anyone what was happening, she would be taken into care.

CARING FOR SALLY

Barnardo's helped Sally by arranging for a home help to come and do the housework and look after Sally's mum.

This gave Sally more time to catch up on her sleep, her school work and do things she enjoys like netball and reading. Barnardo's also introduced Sally to other young carers, so she could make friends with children who understood her problems. Last year Barnardo's took Sally and her younger brother Darren on holiday to the Lake District with some other young carers.

'Before the home help started coming, I'd lost most of my friends at school. Everyone thought I was boring because I never had time to play with them,' says Sally. 'Now I don't have to feel bad every time I leave mum. I've made new friends and things are a lot better.'

21

The average age of young carers is 12.

WORK WITH HOMELESS FAMILIES

Georgie is 10 and his family is **homeless**. He has no games, books or anything of his own. All his things are stored away. He doesn't go to school, because the head teacher told his mum there was no point in him starting a new term when his family would be moving on again soon. So Georgie never sees his friends now.

Georgie longs for a proper home, with his own room, a proper bathroom and a garden. But this could take years to find. So for now, the council has found Georgie and his family some space in a run-down hotel. Georgie's mum, three brothers, his sister and dog called Scraggy all share two rooms.

A third of children living in temporary housing have no school to go to.

> 'The only place to play when you live in a hotel is on the stairs or in the corridors, but then you get shouted at when you make a noise,' says Georgie. Georgie can't wait until he has some space and a garden in which Scraggy, his dog, can play.

< Georgie's mum gives him and his sister lessons at home. They do this in the kitchen, which they share with all the other people who live in the hotel. 'You never get any peace and quiet,' says 15-year-old Siobhan.

NO SPACE

'It's a dump here and there's no space,' says Georgie. 'I share a bed with my brother, who is a security guard. I go to bed when he gets up to work nights. I get so bored it drives me mad and I get told off if I play in the corridor.'

'There are lots of frightening people living here and we have to share our kitchen and bathroom with them,' says Georgie. 'Some of them are on drugs and shout a lot. They scare me.'

OTHER PROJECTS

Barnardo's runs around 30 projects for homeless teenagers and families. Some find or provide somewhere to live for young people. Some help families like Georgie's.

Barnardo's Families in Temporary Accommodation project is helping Georgie's family find a proper home. Georgie will then be able to settle in a new area and go to a new school.

'I can't wait for Barnardo's to find us a new home,' says Georgie. 'I'll have my own room, my own things and go to school, where I will be able to see my mates again. It's going to be brill!'

There are 73,000 families in the UK living in temporary housing.

WORK WITH FOSTERING

There are many children who cannot live with their families. Sometimes it is because their mum or dad has died. There are also children who are taken away from their families for their own safety, to protect them from violence or ill-treatment.

Not being able to stay at home with their mum or dad is very painful for children. So Barnardo's does its best to find them new families.

IAN'S STORY

When Ian was a little boy, he couldn't live with his mum. Barnardo's arranged for him to live with a new family. This is called **fostering**. Ian's foster mum Jean says: 'Ian was six when he came to live with us and was very shy. But he soon settled down and we wouldn't be without him now. Ian is one of the family.'

When children can't be with their parents they often live with another family or in a children's home. This is known as being *in care*. Ian was in a children's home when he was very young, but now he lives with his foster mother, Jean.

24

47,000 children and young people in the UK are in care.

NEW FAMILY

If Ian hadn't been fostered by Jean and her family through Barnardo's, he may have grown up in care and never had a mum or dad to care for him.

'This is my home,' says Ian, who is now 17. 'I don't like to think what would have happened to me if I hadn't come here. Mum (Jean) is great and has seen me through a lot.'

Ian was fostered through Barnardo's Homefinding project in Essex, one of many fostering and **adoption** projects run by the charity.

▶ **'Ian is one of the family,' says Jean. Unfortunately for Ian, it means he has to do chores and help out around the house – just like everyone else!**

Barnardo's runs 33 fostering and adoption projects in the UK.

YOUNG PEOPLE'S SOCIAL ATTITUDES SURVEY

Is it all right to smack children? How would you stop crime? What should children learn at school? Every year the answers to these questions are put together in a **survey** called British Social Attitudes. The survey tells us what's important to people and how they would change things to make the world a better place. But no one ever asked children for their views, until now.

Barnardo's recently brought out the very first Young People's Social Attitudes Survey. It spoke to hundreds of children and teenagers and asked them lots of questions about crime, their families, schools and the world about them. Barnardo's discovered that teenagers do care about others and are very upset by crime, divorce and violence – despite what many people think.

▼ **The survey was launched at a party at Planet Hollywood in London. Pop bands Ultimate Kaos and Upside Down were there to give their support. So was TV personality Gaby Roslin.**

580 young people were interviewed for the Young People's Social Attitudes survey.

THE RESULTS

The survey discovered these facts about young people:

Racism
- nine out of ten believe British society is racist toward black and Asian people

Housework
- nearly eight out of ten believe men and women, boys and girls should share the housework

Schools
- three-quarters believe children should have some say about what they're taught in schools

Bullying
- eight out of ten would report bullying at school

Honesty
- seven out of ten would hand a £100 note to the police if they found it on the street

Safety
- a third feel unsafe going out on their own after dark

Crime
- nearly eight out of ten believe more discipline in school and in families would help reduce crime

What would your views be on these things? What do your friends think?

▶ 'It's important that people listen to what young people have to say,' said the lead singer of Ultimate Kaos. 'We have an important contribution to make to the world.'

▲ Gaby Roslin had the chance to ask lots of teenagers from Barnardo's about their views on schools, crime and families.

The young people interviewed for the survey were aged 12 to 19 years.

VISION FOR THE FUTURE

Children are the future. When you grow up, you will shape the world you live in. You will decide what laws should be passed, who should be Prime Minister and how taxes should be spent.

LISTENING TO CHILDREN

But Barnardo's doesn't believe children should have to wait until they are grown up to make decisions. After all, no one knows more about the problems children face today, than children themselves! Barnardo's believes children should be listened to now.

YOUNG PEOPLE'S CHARTER

Barnardo's recently published a Young People's Charter, which says that the government should always ask children and young people for their views before they pass laws that will affect them. The Charter also says that every child and young person has the right to support, education and a good home as they grow up. They should also have decent job training and a proper job when they leave school.

The Charter was written with the help of hundreds of children and young people that Barnardo's works with. Here are some of their views. How would you make the world a better place if you were asked?

▲ 'I would like everyone to have enough food to eat and no one to have to go hungry.'

Young people believe more should be spent on education and job training in the UK.

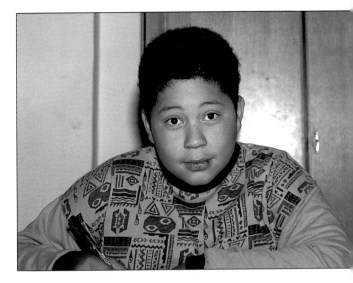

'I want to be able to earn enough money when I grow up to buy mum a big house so she can have her own room and not be bothered by my noisy brothers. I would like a smart car, too.'

'I would like to be able to go down the street with my sister, without everyone staring at us.'

'People should stop blaming teenagers for everything that goes wrong. We get blamed for crime, violence, the lot. It's not our fault. I want to live in a nice world as much as everyone else.'

'All children should have somewhere nice to play, like a garden or park. It is horrible having to live in a flat all the time.'

29

The Charter says that young people should contribute to new laws that affect them.

FURTHER INFORMATION

If you require any further information about Barnardo's please contact:
Barnardo's, Communications, Tanners Lane, Barkingside, Ilford, Essex IG6 1QG
Telephone: 0181 550 8822 Fax: 0181 550 0429

If you would be interested in raising money to help Barnardo's work please contact your nearest regional office listed below:

Central
Barnardo's, Brooklands,
Great Cornbow, Halesowen, West
Midlands B63 3AB
Telephone: 0121 550 5271/6
Fax: 0121 550 2594

London and East Anglia
Barnardo's, Tanners Lane, Barkingside,
Ilford, Essex IG6 1QG
Telephone: 0181 550 8822
Fax: 0181 551 6870

Northern Ireland
Barnardo's, 542–544 Upper
Newtownards Road, Belfast BT4 3HE
Telephone: 01232 672366
Fax: 01232 672399

Northern
Barnardo's, Four Gables, Clarence
Road, Horsforth, Leeds, LS18 4LB
Telephone: 0113 259 1070
Fax: 0113 258 0098

Scotland
Barnardo's, 235 Corstorphine Road,
Edinburgh EH12 7AR
Telephone: 0131 334 9893
Fax: 0131 316 4008

Southern
Barnardo's, Lynnem House,
Victoria Way, Burgess Hill,
West Sussex RH15 9NF
Telephone: 01444 871643
Fax: 01444 871032

Wales and West Country
Barnardo's, 11–15 Columbus Walk,
Brigantine Place, Atlantic Wharf,
Cardiff CF1 5BZ
Telephone: 01222 493387
Fax: 01222 489802

Registered Office
Barnardo's,
Tanners Lane, Barkingside, Ilford,
Essex IG6 1QG
Telephone: 0181 550 8822
Fax: 0181 551 6870

Registration no: 61625 England
Charity registration number: 216250

PATRONS
Her Majesty The Queen
Her Majesty Queen Elizabeth The
Queen Mother

GLOSSARY

adoption when a child or young person lives with a new family permanently and their birth parents hand over all responsibilities

AIDS this stands for Auto Immune Deficiency Syndrome, a condition which makes people less able to fight off ordinary illnesses or get better from them. People die of AIDS-related illnesses.

carers people who look after someone ill or disabled. Some care for a few hours or days a month to give their family a rest; some carers are related to the sick or disabled person and care for them all the time.

depressed feeling very miserable and seeing no hope for the future – sometimes because something serious has gone wrong, or sometimes for no reason at all

disability not being able to use part of the body or mind to its full power, maybe because the muscles have not developed properly, or because the brain is not able to learn as quickly or in the same way as other people

dysentery a serious disease often caught by people drinking dirty water

fostering when a child or young person stays with a new family because they cannot live with their mum or dad

fund-raising appeal collecting money for charity by holding special events like sponsored walks or jumble sales

homeless people with nowhere at all to live, who sleep on the streets, on friends' floors or in empty buildings; or people who live for a short while in unsuitable flats or bed and breakfast hotels because there are not enough affordable, proper homes

in care children who cannot live with their families, who are the responsibility of the local council and are cared for by other families or in large homes with other children

lobbying trying to affect and change plans and laws that are being drawn up by talking to Members of Parliament. People who lobby are known as lobbyists.

media newspapers, magazines, radio, television, satellite and other ways of communicating with a large number of people

multiple sclerosis a disease that attacks the nervous system and can make it difficult to move about, speak, see and control the muscles

physiotherapist a trained person who helps people with injuries or disabilities develop strength and movement in their bodies

poverty not having enough money to buy the basic necessities of life such as food, heating and clothes

survey a way of finding out what people think by asking a group of people questions

tuberculosis a disease which affects the lungs, often caught by people living in damp and cold conditions

31

INDEX